SCHOLASTIC

MW00991648

Math Games
to Master Basic Skills
FRACTIONS & DECIMALS

by Denise Kiernan

Dedication
For Joe

Edited by Immacula A. Rhodes
Cover design by Jason Robinson
Interior illustrations by Teresa Anderko
Interior design by Sydney Wright

ISBN-13: 978-0-439-51772-0
ISBN-10: 0-439-51772-9

Copyright © 2007 by Denise Kiernan.
Published by Scholastic Inc.
All rights reserved.
Printed in the U.S.A.

2 3 4 5 6 7 8 9 10   40   14 13 12 11 10 09 08 07

NEW YORK • TORONTO • LONDON • AUCKLAND • SYDNEY **Teaching**
MEXICO CITY • NEW DELHI • HONG KONG • BUENOS AIRES *Resources*

Contents

Introduction

Math Games to Master Basic Skills: Fractions & Decimals provides fun, familiar games that help students master concepts related to fractions and decimals. The games in this book, variations of well-known childhood games such as Bingo, War!, Go Fish!, Concentration, Tic-Tac-Toe, and Checkers, will engage and motivate students while reinforcing their ability to fluently compute with commonly used fractions and decimals.

The National Council of Teachers of Mathematics (NCTM) defines computational fluency as the "connection between conceptual understanding and computational proficiency." Learning the relationship between fractions and decimals plays a key role in helping students develop strategies to successfully work with each type of representation. You can use these math games to increase students' fluency in using fractions and decimals and help equip them with essential tools to perform higher-level operations with these representations. The games are ideal for students who need extra reinforcement and repeated practice to strengthen their mastery of concepts related to fractions and decimals.

In *Math Games to Master Basic Skills: Fractions & Decimals*, you'll find the materials needed to play the different versions of each game. All you need to supply are the game markers—readily available items such as buttons, plastic counters, or small paper squares. All the games are easy to assemble and can be tailored to fit the needs of individual students, small or large groups, or the entire class.

There are a variety of ways you can use these versatile games with students. Invite students to use the games in learning centers, during free-choice time, before or after school, as class warm-ups, or when they have finished other tasks. You can also send the games home for students to play with family and friends. The variation for each game suggests an additional way to use elements of the game to build and reinforce students' skills and interest.

Math Games to Master Basic Skills: Fractions & Decimals is the perfect tool to help your students master concepts related to fractions and decimals—all-important skills that will put them on the road to math success in future years!

How to Use This Book

Math Games to Master Basic Skills: Fractions & Decimals includes the following:

* An introduction page for each of the six games (pages 8–13): The information on this page includes the game objective, number of players, different versions for playing the game to reinforce addition and subtraction with fractions or decimals, the materials needed, and directions on how to play the game. For all the games except Checkers, variations are provided to suggest additional ways to use the games to build and reinforce students' skills and interest. A challenge activity is also included for each game to help students develop an understanding of the relationship between fractions and decimals.

✳ Reproducible game boards for Bingo and Tic-Tac-Toe (pages 14–15): Each of the game boards contains blank boxes so that you can customize them to target the specific skills you'd like students to work on. Directions for preparing the Bingo game boards are found on page 6. By preparing the game boards in advance, you'll have them ready to use anytime students have an opportunity to play them.

✳ Reproducible game cards (pages 16–36): The game cards are essential components of all the games except Checkers. Each group of game cards represents two or more common fraction families. For most of the fraction families, you'll find a separate set of cards for each of the following:

- fractions that belong to the targeted fraction families
- decimal equivalents of the fractions in the targeted fraction families
- addition problems that feature fractions with like denominators
- addition problems for the decimal equivalents of the fraction addition problems above
- subtraction problems that feature fractions with like denominators
- subtraction problems for the decimal equivalents of the fraction problems above

The exception to the above is that there are no game cards for the decimal equivalents of the $\frac{1}{3}$, $\frac{1}{6}$, and $\frac{1}{9}$ fraction families. To use the game cards, simply decide which skill you'd like to focus on in a game. Then locate the corresponding game cards and prepare them as directed for the selected game (see pages 6–7). In general, the cards labeled with individual fractions can be used with the addition or subtraction problem cards that belong to the same fraction families. Likewise, the cards labeled with individual decimals can be used with the corresponding problem cards featuring decimals. When using the number and problem cards together in games that require matching (such as in Go Fish! and Concentration), you'll find that most but not all of the cards can be used to make matches.

✳ Reproducible caller recording charts (pages 37–43): Laminate and use these charts with the Bingo games in which students add or subtract problems involving fractions or decimals. According to the version of the game being played, the caller selects and calls out specific sums or differences from the chart, marking off each item as it is called. The marked chart can be used to check players' answers and help determine the winner of the game. For durability and reusability, laminate each of the charts. Then have the caller use a wipe-off pen to mark the items. When finished, clean the chart with a paper towel for use again in future games.

✳ Reproducible Checkers game boards (pages 44–47): An easy-to-assemble game board is provided for both fractions and decimals, and contains addition and subtraction problems for each concept. A variety of problems are included to give students practice in converting fractions and adding decimals up to the thousandth place.

Choosing a Version of the Game to Play

There are many different ways you can customize the games in *Math Games to Master Basic Skills: Fractions & Decimals*. This versatility lies in the flexible use of the game boards and game cards. You'll find a "Choose a Version to Play" section for each game that uses the game cards. You can refer to this section to help you decide how students might use the cards to play the game and which game cards to use. For each game, you'll need to target which group of fraction families you want to emphasize. After you become familiar with the different game versions, formats, and materials, you may want to mix and match different fraction families in each game to meet the specific needs of your students or to provide them with more opportunities and challenges to master concepts related to the targeted fraction families. You might also discover other ways to use the games to interest and motivate students.

Here's an example to help you understand how one version of Bingo might be played: Let's say you want players to solve problems that involve adding fractions with like denominators from the $\frac{1}{2}$, $\frac{1}{4}$, and $\frac{1}{8}$ fraction families. For this version, players will use the prepared decimal Bingo game cards that feature problems for this particular group of fractions (label the game boards with this information). The caller will use the corresponding caller recording chart on page 37. To play, the caller calls out sums for the problems on the caller recording chart. Then players search their game boards for addition problems that equal the named sums.

For your convenience, the following chart is provided as a reference to help you locate game cards or caller recording charts for specific fraction families or decimal equivalents.

Fraction Family	Fractions (Page)	Decimals (Page)
Game Cards: $\frac{1}{2}$, $\frac{1}{4}$, and $\frac{1}{8}$ Fraction Families	16	17
Addition	18	19
Subtraction	20	21
Game Cards: $\frac{1}{5}$ and $\frac{1}{10}$ Fraction Families	22	23
Addition	24	25
Subtraction	26	27
Game Cards: $\frac{1}{3}$, $\frac{1}{6}$, and $\frac{1}{9}$ Fraction Families	28	
Addition	29	
Subtraction	30	
Game Cards: $\frac{1}{100}$ and $\frac{1}{1000}$ Fraction Families	31	32
Addition	33	34
Subtraction	35	36
Caller Recording Chart: $\frac{1}{2}$, $\frac{1}{4}$, and $\frac{1}{8}$ Fraction Families		
Addition	37	37
Subtraction	38	38
Caller Recording Chart: $\frac{1}{5}$ and $\frac{1}{10}$ Fraction Families		
Addition	39	39
Subtraction	40	40
Caller Recording Chart: $\frac{1}{3}$, $\frac{1}{6}$, and $\frac{1}{9}$ Fraction Families		
Addition	41	
Subtraction	41	
Caller Recording Chart: $\frac{1}{100}$ and $\frac{1}{1000}$ Fraction Families		
Addition	42	42
Subtraction	43	43

How to Prepare and Use the Games

The game cards on pages 16–36 can be used to play all the games in the book except Checkers. For Bingo, the game cards are glued onto the Bingo game boards. The Tic-Tac-Toe game board is used as a placeholder for the game cards. In War!, Go Fish!, and Concentration, the cards serve as individual playing cards. You'll need to provide game markers for Bingo, Tic-Tac-Toe, and Checkers. Readily available items such as plastic counting chips, buttons, or small paper squares work well as game markers. Follow the directions below to prepare each game for use.

Bingo

By creating your own Bingo board games, you have the flexibility to customize each game to fit students' needs. You can focus on your choice of fraction families or decimals, or a specific operation with fractions or decimals, such as addition or subtraction. You can also decide whether you want to make enough game boards for whole-class use, large or small groups, or pairs. Solicit the help of students or volunteers to create a class supply of the game boards for the different fraction families. Or have individual students make their own game boards that feature the specific fractions they need to work on.

To prepare the game:

1. For a class supply of the game boards, choose the version of the game students will play, the mathematical operation, and the fraction families you want to feature. Then copy a game board on page 14 for each student. Also copy the game cards that feature the selected fact families (refer to the chart on page 5). You'll need two pages of cards for every three students.

2. Distribute the game boards. Have students color the border of their game boards, circle "Fractions" or "Decimals," and write the fraction families on the line.

3. Give every three students two pages of game cards. Have them cut out and place the 48 cards facedown in a random array. Then ask students to pick 16 cards each. Have them glue each card faceup on a blank space on their game board.

4. Collect and laminate all the game boards and the corresponding caller recording charts for the fraction families featured on the game boards. Cut out all the game pieces.

5. Store the game pieces in a large resealable plastic bag. Label the bag with the skill featured on the game boards. Also include a wipe-off pen and paper towels.

To mix it up a bit, you might want to create game boards that feature different combinations of the fraction families. If you do this, be sure to write the skills on the game boards and storage bag, and include copies of all the related caller recording charts.

War!, Go Fish!, and Concentration

To prepare for these games, choose the version you want students to play and the fraction families you'd like to reinforce. Refer to the chart on page 5 to locate the desired cards. Use one set of cards (24 cards) to play War! To play Concentration, select 12 cards from one set of cards and the corresponding 12 cards from another set (such as 12 subtraction cards for fractions and the corresponding subtraction cards for decimals). Similarly, use the corresponding sets of cards for fractions and decimals to play Go Fish! Then copy, laminate, and cut out the cards, and the game's ready to be played—it's that simple! You can store the game cards for each game in a resealable plastic bag labeled with the name of the game and the featured skills.

Tic-Tac-Toe

Choose the version that you'd like students to play. Then select the game cards that correspond to the fraction families you want to feature (refer to the chart on page 5). Copy, laminate, and cut out the game cards and the Tic-Tac-Toe game board on page 15. Store all the game pieces in a large resealable plastic bag labeled with the name of the game and the targeted skills.

Checkers

To prepare each Checkers game board, you'll need a 12- by 18-inch sheet of construction paper and glue. Copy and cut out the two parts for the game board (either pages 44–45 or 46–47), glue them together where indicated, and glue the entire game board to the construction paper. When completed, laminate the game board. To make game markers, laminate two half-sheets of paper, each in a different color. Cut out 12 one-inch squares from each color. To store, label a resealable plastic bag with the name of the game. Place the markers in the bag along with a wipe-off pen and paper towels. Then attach the bag to the game board with a paper clip.

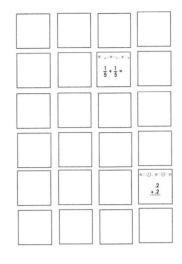

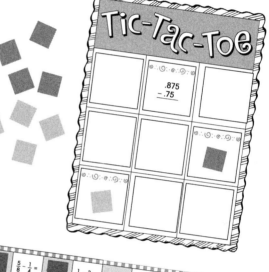

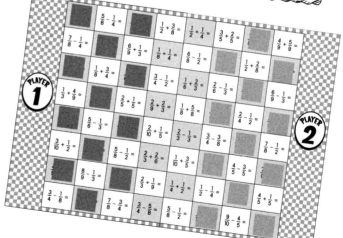

To introduce the different versions of each game, play the game with students or assist them as they play. For games that require turn-taking, help students establish a method for determining the order in which they will take turns, such as by taking turns in the order of their birthdays.

Bingo

Choose a Version to Play

▲ Fractions: Use the targeted fraction addition or subtraction cards
on the game boards and the corresponding caller recording chart on
pages 37–43 (the caller calls out the answers circled on the chart).

◆ Decimals: Use the targeted decimal addition or subtraction cards
on the game boards and the corresponding caller recording chart on
pages 37–43 (the caller calls out the answers circled on the chart).

Materials

• 1 game board per player
• Caller recording charts
• 12 game markers per player
• Wipe-off pen
• Paper towels

How to Play

1. Each player selects a game board and takes 12 game markers.

2. The caller calls out the circled answer for any item shown on
the caller recording chart. Then he or she marks that item with the
wipe-off pen.

3. Players check their game boards to see if any spaces show
a match to the called item. (They might solve the problems on
paper first.) If a player finds a match, he or she places a marker
on the space. The player may place a marker on only one space
for each item called, even if there is more than one match on
the game board.

4. Play continues with the caller calling out one item at a
time and players searching their game boards for matches.
The first player to cover four spaces in a row—across, down, or
diagonally—calls "Bingo!" Then the player and caller compare
each answer on the game board to the marked items on the
caller recording charts to check for correctness. If all the answers
are correct, the player wins the game.

Challenge

To reinforce the equivalent relationship between fractions and decimals,
give each player a game board featuring individual fractions. Have the caller
use the corresponding decimal game cards as caller cards. For example,
if the caller calls .5, players cover $\frac{1}{2}$, $\frac{2}{4}$, or $\frac{4}{8}$ on their game boards. Players
might also use game boards with addition or subtraction problems involving
fractions while the caller calls the problems (instead of the circled answers)
from the corresponding decimal equivalent caller recording charts.

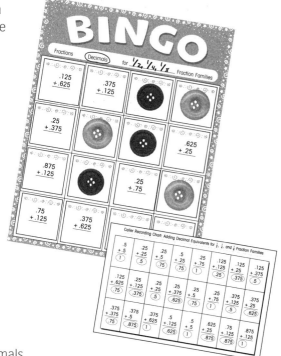

Variation

Instead of four in a
row, have players
cover all the spaces
on their game
boards to win.

8

War!

Choose a Version to Play

▲ Fractions: Use the fraction addition or subtraction cards for the targeted fact families.

◆ Decimals: Use the decimal addition or subtraction cards for the targeted fact families.

Materials

• 24 game cards

How to Play

1. One player shuffles the cards and deals them evenly between the players. Each player stacks his or her cards facedown.

2. Each player turns over the top card on his or her stack. Then each player announces the answer to the problem on his or her card. The player with the card that equals the higher value takes both cards and puts them facedown on the bottom of his or her stack.

   ✳ If both cards have the same value, the players call out "War!" Then each player turns over the next card in his or her stack. The player with the war card that has the higher value wins the war. That player collects all the cards in play.

   ✳ If both war cards have the same value, players continue the war by turning over the next card in their stacks. The war ends when one player turns over a card with a higher value than the other player's card.

3. Play continues until one player collects all the cards and ends the game. The player with all the cards wins the game.

Challenge

To help emphasize the equivalent relationship between fractions and decimals, use a set of corresponding fraction and decimal cards (such as from the $\frac{1}{5}$ and $\frac{1}{10}$ fraction families). Explain that in this version, players will compare fractions to fractions, decimals to decimals, and fractions to decimals. In each round, the player with the higher value card wins the round.

Variation

For 3–4 players, use two sets of game cards for the fraction families of your choice. Deal the 48 game cards evenly among the players. Whenever two or more players turn over cards that have the same value, each of those players participates in the war to break the tie.

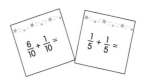

Go Fish!

Choose a Version to Play

▲ Fractions: Use a set of 24 fraction problem cards and the 24 fraction number cards for the corresponding fraction families.

◆ Decimals: Use a set of 24 decimal problem cards and the 24 decimal number cards for the corresponding fraction families.

Materials

• 48 game cards

How to Play

1. One player shuffles the cards, deals five cards to each player, and places the stack facedown on the table.

2. The first player checks his or her cards for matches. A match can be made if a problem card has the same value as a number card (such as $\frac{1}{6} + \frac{2}{6}$ and $\frac{3}{6}$), two problem cards have the same answer (such as $\frac{2}{9} + \frac{3}{9}$ and $\frac{4}{9} + \frac{1}{9}$), or two number cards have the same value (such as $\frac{1}{3}$ and $\frac{2}{6}$). If the player has two or more matching cards, he or she shows the match to the other players and places it on the table.

3. The first player then calls out a problem or number card in his or her hand. The player names another player and asks him or her for any matching cards.

　✳ If the named player has one or more matching cards, he or she must give all of those cards to the asking player. That player then lays the new match on the table and takes another turn.

　✳ If the named player does not have any matching cards, he or she says "Go Fish." Then the asking player takes the top card in the stack, adds it to his or her hand, and the turn ends.

4. Players continue to take turns. The game ends when a player uses all the cards in his or her hand or no more matches can be made. To score, each player counts the sets off matching cards he or she has on the table. The player with the most sets of matches wins.

Challenge

Use 24 fraction problem cards and the 24 corresponding decimal problem cards. To play, a player calls out a problem and asks another player for an equivalent form of the problem. For example, a player might call out .5 − .25. If the asked player holds a card with $\frac{2}{4} - \frac{1}{4}$ or $\frac{4}{8} - \frac{2}{8}$, he or she gives the card to the asking player.

OBJECTIVE

To solve fraction or decimal problems and be the player with the most sets of matching cards at the end of the game

Variation

Make two copies of the same set of fraction problem cards. To use, players request cards by naming the answer to the problem on a card in his or her hand.

Concentration

Choose a Version to Play

▲ Fractions: Use 12 fraction addition or subtraction cards and the 12 corresponding fraction number cards.

◆ Decimals: Use 12 decimal addition or subtraction cards and the 12 corresponding decimal number cards.

Materials

• 24 game cards

How to Play

1. Players place the game cards facedown on the table in a four-by-six array.

2. The first player turns over any two cards and checks to see if the cards form a match. A match can be made only when a player turns over a problem card and a number card. If the answer to the problem equals the number on the other card, a match is made. If a player turns over two problem cards or two number cards, the turn ends and the player returns the cards facedown to their positions on the table.

　✷ If the player finds a match, he or she keeps the cards and takes another turn.

　✷ If the player does not find a match, he or she returns the cards facedown to the table and the turn ends.

3. Players continue to take turns until all the possible matches have been made. At the end of the game, each player counts his or her matches. The player with the most matches wins the game.

Challenge

Play this version to reinforce the equivalent relationship between fractions and decimals. Place 12 fraction number cards and the corresponding 12 decimal number cards facedown on the table. Players turn over two cards at a time. If both cards show either fractions or decimals, the player returns the cards to the table and the turn ends. If one card shows a fraction and the other a decimal, the player decides whether or not the two numbers are equivalent to each other (such as $\frac{3}{100}$ and .03). If so, the player keeps the cards and takes another turn. If not, the player returns the cards to the table.

OBJECTIVE

To match fraction or decimal problems to the correct answers and be the player with the most matches at the end of the game

Variation

To add interest, tell players that matches can also be made if two problem cards have the same answer (such as $\frac{5}{10} - \frac{3}{10}$ and $\frac{6}{10} - \frac{4}{10}$) or two number cards have the same value (such as $\frac{1}{5}$ and $\frac{2}{10}$).

Tic-Tac-Toe

Choose a Version to Play

▲ Fractions: Use two sets of fraction problem cards (two copies of the same set of cards can be used, or two different sets of cards).

◆ Decimals: Use two sets of decimal problem cards (two copies of the same set of cards can be used, or two different sets of cards).

Materials

- 48 game cards
- Tic-Tac-Toe game board (page 15)
- Set of 5 game markers per player, each set a different color

How to Play

1. One player shuffles the cards and then places one card facedown on each square on the game board. The player sets the remaining stack of cards aside for later use. Each player selects a set of game markers.

2. The first player turns over a card, reads the problem, and gives the answer. If the player answers correctly, he or she places a marker on that card and the turn ends. If the player's answer is incorrect, the turn ends. The second player may choose to answer that problem or turn over another card. If he or she chooses to turn over another card, the first one is returned facedown on its space.

3. Players continue taking turns until one player places his or her markers on three cards in a row—across, down, or diagonally—or until all the cards have been turned over and the problems answered correctly. If a player marks three cards in a row, he or she wins the round. If neither player marks three cards in a row, the round is a tie.

4. At the end of the round, players collect their markers and remove the cards from the game board. They then use nine more cards from the stack to set up the game board for another round of play. (There are enough cards for players to play five rounds of Tic-Tac-Toe, with three cards remaining unused.)

Challenge

After solving a problem, have each player tell the equivalent form of the answer. For example, the answer to .25 + .25 is .5, and its equivalent fraction is $\frac{1}{2}$.

OBJECTIVE

To correctly answer fraction or decimal problems and be the first player to cover three squares in a row on the Tic-Tac-Toe game board

Variation

Have players answer each problem with the equivalent form of the same operation. For example, for $\frac{3}{8} - \frac{1}{8}$, the player answers with .375 − .125.

Checkers

Choose a Version to Play

▲ Fractions: Use the fraction Checkers game board (pages 44–45).

◆ Decimals: Use the decimal Checkers game board (pages 46–47).

Materials

- Checkers game board
- Set of 12 game markers per player, each set a different color
- Wipe-off pen
- Paper towels

OBJECTIVE

To solve problems involving fractions or decimals and be the first player to either capture all the opponent's markers or prevent him or her from making any more moves

How to Play

1. Each player selects one side of the game board and a set of markers. The player places a marker on each shaded space on the first three rows of his or her side of the game board.

2. The first player moves one of his or her markers forward diagonally to a shaded space without a marker. The player reads and answers the problem on that space. If correct, the player leaves the marker on the space and the turn ends. If incorrect, the player returns the marker to its original space and the turn ends.

3. Players take turns moving their markers. When a player moves to a space that touches the corner of a space holding the opponent's marker, the player may try to capture that marker—but only if the space on the opposite corner does not hold a marker. To do this, the player jumps his or her marker over the opponent's marker to the space without a marker. Then the player answers the problem on that space and all the problems on the surrounding white spaces.

   ✳ If the player answers all the problems correctly, he or she captures the opponent's marker by removing it from the board. Then the turn ends.

   ✳ If the player does not answer all the problems correctly, the capture does not take place. The player moves his or her marker back to its original space, and the turn ends.

4. When a player moves a marker to the last row on the opposite side of the game board, and then correctly answers the problem on that space and any surrounding white spaces, the marker may be crowned a king. To do this, the player writes a *K* on the marker. Players may move their kings forward or backward. To capture an opponent's marker with a king, players must follow the capture rule in Step 3.

5. Play continues until one player wins by either capturing all of his or her opponent's markers or preventing the opponent from making any more moves. When finished, players clean their game markers with a paper towel for use again in future games.

BINGO

Fractions   Decimals   for _____ Fraction Families

Math Games to Master Basic Skills: Fractions & Decimals   Scholastic Teaching Resources

Tic-Tac-Toe Game Board

Fraction Game Cards: $\frac{1}{2}$, $\frac{1}{4}$, and $\frac{1}{8}$ Fraction Families

$\frac{1}{2}$	$\frac{2}{2}$	$\frac{1}{4}$	$\frac{2}{4}$
$\frac{3}{4}$	$\frac{3}{4}$	$\frac{4}{4}$	$\frac{1}{8}$
$\frac{1}{8}$	$\frac{1}{8}$	$\frac{2}{8}$	$\frac{2}{8}$
$\frac{3}{8}$	$\frac{3}{8}$	$\frac{4}{8}$	$\frac{4}{8}$
$\frac{5}{8}$	$\frac{5}{8}$	$\frac{6}{8}$	$\frac{6}{8}$
$\frac{7}{8}$	$\frac{7}{8}$	$\frac{8}{8}$	$\frac{8}{8}$

Math Games to Master Basic Skills: Fractions & Decimals Scholastic Teaching Resources

Decimal Game Cards: Equivalents of $\frac{1}{2}$, $\frac{1}{4}$, and $\frac{1}{8}$ Fraction Families

.5	1	.25	.5
.75	.75	1	.125
.125	.125	.25	.25
.375	.375	.5	.5
.625	.625	.75	.75
.875	.875	1	1

$\frac{1}{2} + \frac{1}{2} =$	$\frac{1}{4} + \frac{1}{4} =$	$\frac{1}{4} + \frac{2}{4} =$	$\frac{2}{4} + \frac{1}{4} =$
$\frac{1}{4} + \frac{3}{4} =$	$\frac{1}{8} + \frac{1}{8} =$	$\frac{1}{8} + \frac{2}{8} =$	$\frac{1}{8} + \frac{3}{8} =$
$\frac{1}{8} + \frac{5}{8} =$	$\frac{2}{8} + \frac{1}{8} =$	$\frac{2}{8} + \frac{2}{8} =$	$\frac{2}{8} + \frac{3}{8} =$
$\frac{2}{8} + \frac{4}{8} =$	$\frac{2}{8} + \frac{6}{8} =$	$\frac{3}{8} + \frac{1}{8} =$	$\frac{3}{8} + \frac{2}{8} =$
$\frac{3}{8} + \frac{3}{8} =$	$\frac{3}{8} + \frac{4}{8} =$	$\frac{3}{8} + \frac{5}{8} =$	$\frac{4}{8} + \frac{1}{8} =$
$\frac{4}{8} + \frac{4}{8} =$	$\frac{5}{8} + \frac{2}{8} =$	$\frac{6}{8} + \frac{1}{8} =$	$\frac{7}{8} + \frac{1}{8} =$

Math Games to Master Basic Skills: Fractions & Decimals Scholastic Teaching Resources

Decimal Game Cards: Adding Equivalents of $\frac{1}{2}$, $\frac{1}{4}$, and $\frac{1}{8}$ Fraction Families

.5 +.5	.25 +.25	.25 +.5	.5 +.25
.25 +.75	.125 +.125	.125 +.25	.125 +.375
.125 +.625	.25 +.125	.25 +.25	.25 +.375
.25 +.5	.25 +.75	.375 +.125	.375 +.25
.375 +.375	.375 +.5	.375 +.625	.5 +.125
.5 +.5	.625 +.25	.75 +.125	.875 +.125

Math Games to Master Basic Skills: Fractions & Decimals Scholastic Teaching Resources

19

$\frac{2}{2} - \frac{1}{2} =$	$\frac{3}{4} - \frac{1}{4} =$	$\frac{3}{4} - \frac{2}{4} =$	$\frac{4}{4} - \frac{1}{4} =$
$\frac{8}{8} - \frac{1}{8} =$	$\frac{8}{8} - \frac{2}{8} =$	$\frac{8}{8} - \frac{3}{8} =$	$\frac{8}{8} - \frac{5}{8} =$
$\frac{7}{8} - \frac{1}{8} =$	$\frac{7}{8} - \frac{3}{8} =$	$\frac{7}{8} - \frac{4}{8} =$	$\frac{7}{8} - \frac{6}{8} =$
$\frac{6}{8} - \frac{1}{8} =$	$\frac{6}{8} - \frac{2}{8} =$	$\frac{6}{8} - \frac{4}{8} =$	$\frac{6}{8} - \frac{5}{8} =$
$\frac{5}{8} - \frac{1}{8} =$	$\frac{5}{8} - \frac{3}{8} =$	$\frac{5}{8} - \frac{4}{8} =$	$\frac{4}{8} - \frac{1}{8} =$
$\frac{4}{8} - \frac{2}{8} =$	$\frac{3}{8} - \frac{1}{8} =$	$\frac{3}{8} - \frac{2}{8} =$	$\frac{2}{8} - \frac{1}{8} =$

Math Games to Master Basic Skills: Fractions & Decimals   Scholastic Teaching Resources

Decimal Game Cards: Subtracting With Equivalents of $\frac{1}{2}$, $\frac{1}{4}$, and $\frac{1}{8}$ Fraction Families

$\begin{array}{r} 1 \\ -\ .5 \\ \hline \end{array}$	$\begin{array}{r} .75 \\ -\ .25 \\ \hline \end{array}$	$\begin{array}{r} .75 \\ -\ .5 \\ \hline \end{array}$	$\begin{array}{r} 1 \\ -\ .25 \\ \hline \end{array}$
$\begin{array}{r} 1 \\ -\ .125 \\ \hline \end{array}$	$\begin{array}{r} 1 \\ -\ .25 \\ \hline \end{array}$	$\begin{array}{r} 1 \\ -\ .375 \\ \hline \end{array}$	$\begin{array}{r} 1 \\ -\ .625 \\ \hline \end{array}$
$\begin{array}{r} .875 \\ -\ .125 \\ \hline \end{array}$	$\begin{array}{r} .875 \\ -\ .375 \\ \hline \end{array}$	$\begin{array}{r} .875 \\ -\ .5 \\ \hline \end{array}$	$\begin{array}{r} .875 \\ -\ .75 \\ \hline \end{array}$
$\begin{array}{r} .75 \\ -\ .125 \\ \hline \end{array}$	$\begin{array}{r} .75 \\ -\ .25 \\ \hline \end{array}$	$\begin{array}{r} .75 \\ -\ .5 \\ \hline \end{array}$	$\begin{array}{r} .75 \\ -\ .625 \\ \hline \end{array}$
$\begin{array}{r} .625 \\ -\ .125 \\ \hline \end{array}$	$\begin{array}{r} .625 \\ -\ .375 \\ \hline \end{array}$	$\begin{array}{r} .625 \\ -\ .5 \\ \hline \end{array}$	$\begin{array}{r} .5 \\ -\ .125 \\ \hline \end{array}$
$\begin{array}{r} .5 \\ -\ .25 \\ \hline \end{array}$	$\begin{array}{r} .375 \\ -\ .125 \\ \hline \end{array}$	$\begin{array}{r} .375 \\ -\ .25 \\ \hline \end{array}$	$\begin{array}{r} .25 \\ -\ .125 \\ \hline \end{array}$

$\dfrac{1}{5}$	$\dfrac{1}{5}$	$\dfrac{2}{5}$	$\dfrac{3}{5}$
$\dfrac{4}{5}$	$\dfrac{5}{5}$	$\dfrac{1}{10}$	$\dfrac{1}{10}$
$\dfrac{2}{10}$	$\dfrac{2}{10}$	$\dfrac{3}{10}$	$\dfrac{3}{10}$
$\dfrac{4}{10}$	$\dfrac{4}{10}$	$\dfrac{5}{10}$	$\dfrac{6}{10}$
$\dfrac{6}{10}$	$\dfrac{7}{10}$	$\dfrac{7}{10}$	$\dfrac{8}{10}$
$\dfrac{8}{10}$	$\dfrac{9}{10}$	$\dfrac{9}{10}$	$\dfrac{10}{10}$

Math Games to Master Basic Skills: Fractions & Decimals Scholastic Teaching Resources

Decimal Game Cards: Equivalents of $\frac{1}{5}$ and $\frac{1}{10}$ Fraction Families

.2	.2	.4	.6
.8	1	.1	.1
.2	.2	.3	.3
.4	.4	.5	.6
.6	.7	.7	.8
.8	.9	.9	1

$\dfrac{1}{5} + \dfrac{1}{5} =$	$\dfrac{1}{5} + \dfrac{2}{5} =$	$\dfrac{2}{5} + \dfrac{3}{5} =$	$\dfrac{3}{5} + \dfrac{1}{5} =$
$\dfrac{4}{5} + \dfrac{1}{5} =$	$\dfrac{1}{10} + \dfrac{1}{10} =$	$\dfrac{1}{10} + \dfrac{3}{10} =$	$\dfrac{1}{10} + \dfrac{4}{10} =$
$\dfrac{1}{10} + \dfrac{7}{10} =$	$\dfrac{2}{10} + \dfrac{1}{10} =$	$\dfrac{2}{10} + \dfrac{3}{10} =$	$\dfrac{2}{10} + \dfrac{5}{10} =$
$\dfrac{3}{10} + \dfrac{3}{10} =$	$\dfrac{3}{10} + \dfrac{5}{10} =$	$\dfrac{3}{10} + \dfrac{7}{10} =$	$\dfrac{4}{10} + \dfrac{3}{10} =$
$\dfrac{4}{10} + \dfrac{4}{10} =$	$\dfrac{4}{10} + \dfrac{5}{10} =$	$\dfrac{5}{10} + \dfrac{1}{10} =$	$\dfrac{5}{10} + \dfrac{5}{10} =$
$\dfrac{6}{10} + \dfrac{1}{10} =$	$\dfrac{6}{10} + \dfrac{3}{10} =$	$\dfrac{7}{10} + \dfrac{2}{10} =$	$\dfrac{8}{10} + \dfrac{2}{10} =$

Math Games to Master Basic Skills: Fractions & Decimals Scholastic Teaching Resources

Decimal Game Cards: Adding Equivalents of $\frac{1}{5}$ and $\frac{1}{10}$ Fraction Families

$\begin{array}{r} .2 \\ +.2 \\ \hline \end{array}$	$\begin{array}{r} .2 \\ +.4 \\ \hline \end{array}$	$\begin{array}{r} .4 \\ +.6 \\ \hline \end{array}$	$\begin{array}{r} .6 \\ +.2 \\ \hline \end{array}$
$\begin{array}{r} .8 \\ +.2 \\ \hline \end{array}$	$\begin{array}{r} .1 \\ +.1 \\ \hline \end{array}$	$\begin{array}{r} .1 \\ +.3 \\ \hline \end{array}$	$\begin{array}{r} .1 \\ +.4 \\ \hline \end{array}$
$\begin{array}{r} .1 \\ +.7 \\ \hline \end{array}$	$\begin{array}{r} .2 \\ +.1 \\ \hline \end{array}$	$\begin{array}{r} .2 \\ +.3 \\ \hline \end{array}$	$\begin{array}{r} .2 \\ +.5 \\ \hline \end{array}$
$\begin{array}{r} .3 \\ +.3 \\ \hline \end{array}$	$\begin{array}{r} .3 \\ +.5 \\ \hline \end{array}$	$\begin{array}{r} .3 \\ +.7 \\ \hline \end{array}$	$\begin{array}{r} .4 \\ +.3 \\ \hline \end{array}$
$\begin{array}{r} .4 \\ +.4 \\ \hline \end{array}$	$\begin{array}{r} .4 \\ +.5 \\ \hline \end{array}$	$\begin{array}{r} .5 \\ +.1 \\ \hline \end{array}$	$\begin{array}{r} .5 \\ +.5 \\ \hline \end{array}$
$\begin{array}{r} .6 \\ +.1 \\ \hline \end{array}$	$\begin{array}{r} .6 \\ +.3 \\ \hline \end{array}$	$\begin{array}{r} .7 \\ +.2 \\ \hline \end{array}$	$\begin{array}{r} .8 \\ +.2 \\ \hline \end{array}$

$\frac{4}{5} - \frac{1}{5} =$	$\frac{4}{5} - \frac{2}{5} =$	$\frac{3}{5} - \frac{1}{5} =$	$\frac{3}{5} - \frac{2}{5} =$
$\frac{2}{5} - \frac{1}{5} =$	$\frac{10}{10} - \frac{1}{10} =$	$\frac{9}{10} - \frac{1}{10} =$	$\frac{9}{10} - \frac{2}{10} =$
$\frac{9}{10} - \frac{5}{10} =$	$\frac{9}{10} - \frac{8}{10} =$	$\frac{8}{10} - \frac{2}{10} =$	$\frac{8}{10} - \frac{5}{10} =$
$\frac{8}{10} - \frac{6}{10} =$	$\frac{8}{10} - \frac{7}{10} =$	$\frac{7}{10} - \frac{2}{10} =$	$\frac{7}{10} - \frac{4}{10} =$
$\frac{6}{10} - \frac{2}{10} =$	$\frac{6}{10} - \frac{5}{10} =$	$\frac{5}{10} - \frac{3}{10} =$	$\frac{5}{10} - \frac{4}{10} =$
$\frac{4}{10} - \frac{1}{10} =$	$\frac{4}{10} - \frac{2}{10} =$	$\frac{3}{10} - \frac{1}{10} =$	$\frac{2}{10} - \frac{1}{10} =$

Math Games to Master Basic Skills: Fractions & Decimals Scholastic Teaching Resources

Decimal Game Cards: Subtracting With Equivalents of $\frac{1}{5}$ and $\frac{1}{10}$ Fraction Families

$\begin{array}{r} .8 \\ -\ .2 \\ \hline \end{array}$	$\begin{array}{r} .8 \\ -\ .4 \\ \hline \end{array}$	$\begin{array}{r} .6 \\ -\ .2 \\ \hline \end{array}$	$\begin{array}{r} .6 \\ -\ .4 \\ \hline \end{array}$
$\begin{array}{r} .4 \\ -\ .2 \\ \hline \end{array}$	$\begin{array}{r} 1 \\ -\ .1 \\ \hline \end{array}$	$\begin{array}{r} .9 \\ -\ .1 \\ \hline \end{array}$	$\begin{array}{r} .9 \\ -\ .2 \\ \hline \end{array}$
$\begin{array}{r} .9 \\ -\ .5 \\ \hline \end{array}$	$\begin{array}{r} .9 \\ -\ .8 \\ \hline \end{array}$	$\begin{array}{r} .8 \\ -\ .2 \\ \hline \end{array}$	$\begin{array}{r} .8 \\ -\ .5 \\ \hline \end{array}$
$\begin{array}{r} .8 \\ -\ .6 \\ \hline \end{array}$	$\begin{array}{r} .8 \\ -\ .7 \\ \hline \end{array}$	$\begin{array}{r} .7 \\ -\ .2 \\ \hline \end{array}$	$\begin{array}{r} .7 \\ -\ .4 \\ \hline \end{array}$
$\begin{array}{r} .6 \\ -\ .2 \\ \hline \end{array}$	$\begin{array}{r} .6 \\ -\ .5 \\ \hline \end{array}$	$\begin{array}{r} .5 \\ -\ .3 \\ \hline \end{array}$	$\begin{array}{r} .5 \\ -\ .4 \\ \hline \end{array}$
$\begin{array}{r} .4 \\ -\ .1 \\ \hline \end{array}$	$\begin{array}{r} .4 \\ -\ .2 \\ \hline \end{array}$	$\begin{array}{r} .3 \\ -\ .1 \\ \hline \end{array}$	$\begin{array}{r} .2 \\ -\ .1 \\ \hline \end{array}$

$\frac{1}{3}$	$\frac{2}{3}$	$\frac{3}{3}$	$\frac{1}{6}$
$\frac{2}{6}$	$\frac{3}{6}$	$\frac{3}{6}$	$\frac{4}{6}$
$\frac{4}{6}$	$\frac{5}{6}$	$\frac{6}{6}$	$\frac{1}{9}$
$\frac{2}{9}$	$\frac{3}{9}$	$\frac{3}{9}$	$\frac{4}{9}$
$\frac{4}{9}$	$\frac{5}{9}$	$\frac{5}{9}$	$\frac{6}{9}$
$\frac{6}{9}$	$\frac{7}{9}$	$\frac{8}{9}$	$\frac{9}{9}$

Math Games to Master Basic Skills: Fractions & Decimals Scholastic Teaching Resources

Fraction Game Cards: Adding With Like Denominators for $\frac{1}{3}$, $\frac{1}{6}$, and $\frac{1}{9}$ Fraction Families

$\frac{1}{3} + \frac{1}{3} =$	$\frac{2}{3} + \frac{1}{3} =$	$\frac{1}{6} + \frac{1}{6} =$	$\frac{1}{6} + \frac{2}{6} =$
$\frac{1}{6} + \frac{4}{6} =$	$\frac{2}{6} + \frac{2}{6} =$	$\frac{2}{6} + \frac{3}{6} =$	$\frac{3}{6} + \frac{1}{6} =$
$\frac{4}{6} + \frac{2}{6} =$	$\frac{5}{6} + \frac{1}{6} =$	$\frac{1}{9} + \frac{1}{9} =$	$\frac{1}{9} + \frac{2}{9} =$
$\frac{1}{9} + \frac{3}{9} =$	$\frac{1}{9} + \frac{5}{9} =$	$\frac{2}{9} + \frac{3}{9} =$	$\frac{2}{9} + \frac{4}{9} =$
$\frac{2}{9} + \frac{6}{9} =$	$\frac{3}{9} + \frac{1}{9} =$	$\frac{3}{9} + \frac{3}{9} =$	$\frac{3}{9} + \frac{5}{9} =$
$\frac{4}{9} + \frac{1}{9} =$	$\frac{4}{9} + \frac{5}{9} =$	$\frac{5}{9} + \frac{2}{9} =$	$\frac{6}{9} + \frac{3}{9} =$

$\frac{2}{3} - \frac{1}{3} =$	$\frac{3}{3} - \frac{1}{3} =$	$\frac{6}{6} - \frac{1}{6} =$	$\frac{6}{6} - \frac{2}{6} =$
$\frac{5}{6} - \frac{1}{6} =$	$\frac{5}{6} - \frac{2}{6} =$	$\frac{4}{6} - \frac{1}{6} =$	$\frac{3}{6} - \frac{1}{6} =$
$\frac{2}{6} - \frac{1}{6} =$	$\frac{9}{9} - \frac{1}{9} =$	$\frac{9}{9} - \frac{4}{9} =$	$\frac{9}{9} - \frac{5}{9} =$
$\frac{8}{9} - \frac{1}{9} =$	$\frac{8}{9} - \frac{2}{9} =$	$\frac{8}{9} - \frac{4}{9} =$	$\frac{7}{9} - \frac{1}{9} =$
$\frac{7}{9} - \frac{2}{9} =$	$\frac{6}{9} - \frac{1}{9} =$	$\frac{6}{9} - \frac{3}{9} =$	$\frac{5}{9} - \frac{1}{9} =$
$\frac{5}{9} - \frac{2}{9} =$	$\frac{4}{9} - \frac{1}{9} =$	$\frac{4}{9} - \frac{2}{9} =$	$\frac{3}{9} - \frac{2}{9} =$

Math Games to Master Basic Skills: Fractions & Decimals Scholastic Teaching Resources

Fraction Game Cards: $\frac{1}{100}$ and $\frac{1}{1000}$ Fraction Families

$\frac{1}{100}$	$\frac{2}{100}$	$\frac{3}{100}$	$\frac{4}{100}$
$\frac{5}{100}$	$\frac{6}{100}$	$\frac{7}{100}$	$\frac{8}{100}$
$\frac{9}{100}$	$\frac{25}{100}$	$\frac{75}{100}$	$\frac{100}{100}$
$\frac{1}{1000}$	$\frac{2}{1000}$	$\frac{3}{1000}$	$\frac{4}{1000}$
$\frac{5}{1000}$	$\frac{6}{1000}$	$\frac{7}{1000}$	$\frac{8}{1000}$
$\frac{9}{1000}$	$\frac{25}{1000}$	$\frac{75}{1000}$	$\frac{1000}{1000}$

.01	.02	.03	.04
.05	.06	.07	.08
.09	.25	.75	1
.001	.002	.003	.004
.005	.006	.007	.008
.009	.025	.075	1

$\dfrac{1}{100} + \dfrac{1}{100} =$	$\dfrac{1}{100} + \dfrac{3}{100} =$	$\dfrac{2}{100} + \dfrac{1}{100} =$	$\dfrac{2}{100} + \dfrac{5}{100} =$
$\dfrac{3}{100} + \dfrac{2}{100} =$	$\dfrac{3}{100} + \dfrac{4}{100} =$	$\dfrac{4}{100} + \dfrac{2}{100} =$	$\dfrac{5}{100} + \dfrac{3}{100} =$
$\dfrac{6}{100} + \dfrac{3}{100} =$	$\dfrac{7}{100} + \dfrac{1}{100} =$	$\dfrac{8}{100} + \dfrac{1}{100} =$	$\dfrac{25}{100} + \dfrac{75}{100} =$
$\dfrac{1}{1000} + \dfrac{1}{1000} =$	$\dfrac{1}{1000} + \dfrac{3}{1000} =$	$\dfrac{2}{1000} + \dfrac{1}{1000} =$	$\dfrac{2}{1000} + \dfrac{5}{1000} =$
$\dfrac{3}{1000} + \dfrac{2}{1000} =$	$\dfrac{3}{1000} + \dfrac{4}{1000} =$	$\dfrac{4}{1000} + \dfrac{2}{1000} =$	$\dfrac{4}{1000} + \dfrac{5}{1000} =$
$\dfrac{5}{1000} + \dfrac{1}{1000} =$	$\dfrac{5}{1000} + \dfrac{3}{1000} =$	$\dfrac{6}{1000} + \dfrac{2}{1000} =$	$\dfrac{900}{1000} + \dfrac{100}{1000} =$

.01 +.01	.01 +.03	.02 +.01	.02 +.05
.03 +.02	.03 +.04	.04 +.02	.05 +.03
.06 +.03	.07 +.01	.08 +.01	.25 +.75
.001 +.001	.001 +.003	.002 +.001	.002 +.005
.003 +.002	.003 +.004	.004 +.002	.004 +.005
.005 +.001	.005 +.003	.006 +.002	.900 +.100

Math Games to Master Basic Skills: Fractions & Decimals   Scholastic Teaching Resources

$\frac{10}{100} - \frac{1}{100} =$	$\frac{9}{100} - \frac{1}{100} =$	$\frac{9}{100} - \frac{2}{100} =$	$\frac{8}{100} - \frac{2}{100} =$
$\frac{8}{100} - \frac{4}{100} =$	$\frac{7}{100} - \frac{3}{100} =$	$\frac{6}{100} - \frac{1}{100} =$	$\frac{6}{100} - \frac{5}{100} =$
$\frac{5}{100} - \frac{2}{100} =$	$\frac{4}{100} - \frac{3}{100} =$	$\frac{3}{100} - \frac{1}{100} =$	$\frac{2}{100} - \frac{1}{100} =$
$\frac{10}{1000} - \frac{1}{1000} =$	$\frac{9}{1000} - \frac{1}{1000} =$	$\frac{9}{1000} - \frac{3}{1000} =$	$\frac{8}{1000} - \frac{1}{1000} =$
$\frac{8}{1000} - \frac{5}{1000} =$	$\frac{7}{1000} - \frac{2}{1000} =$	$\frac{7}{1000} - \frac{5}{1000} =$	$\frac{6}{1000} - \frac{2}{1000} =$
$\frac{5}{1000} - \frac{2}{1000} =$	$\frac{4}{1000} - \frac{3}{1000} =$	$\frac{3}{1000} - \frac{1}{1000} =$	$\frac{2}{1000} - \frac{1}{1000} =$

Decimal Game Cards: Subtracting With Equivalents of $\frac{1}{100}$ and $\frac{1}{1000}$ Fraction Families

.1 − .01	.09 − .01	.09 − .02	.08 − .02
.08 − .04	.07 − .03	.06 − .01	.06 − .05
.05 − .02	.04 − .03	.03 − .01	.02 − .01
.01 − .001	.009 − .001	.009 − .003	.008 − .001
.008 − .005	.007 − .002	.007 − .005	.006 − .002
.005 − .002	.004 − .003	.003 − .001	.002 − .001

Math Games to Master Basic Skills: Fractions & Decimals Scholastic Teaching Resources

Caller Recording Chart: Adding With Like Denominators for $\frac{1}{2}$, $\frac{1}{4}$, and $\frac{1}{8}$ Fraction Families

$\frac{1}{2} + \frac{1}{2} = \frac{2}{2}$	$\frac{1}{4} + \frac{1}{4} = \frac{2}{4}$	$\frac{1}{4} + \frac{2}{4} = \frac{3}{4}$	$\frac{2}{4} + \frac{1}{4} = \frac{3}{4}$
$\frac{1}{4} + \frac{3}{4} = \frac{4}{4}$	$\frac{1}{8} + \frac{1}{8} = \frac{2}{8}$	$\frac{1}{8} + \frac{2}{8} = \frac{3}{8}$	$\frac{1}{8} + \frac{3}{8} = \frac{4}{8}$
$\frac{1}{8} + \frac{5}{8} = \frac{6}{8}$	$\frac{2}{8} + \frac{1}{8} = \frac{3}{8}$	$\frac{2}{8} + \frac{2}{8} = \frac{4}{8}$	$\frac{2}{8} + \frac{3}{8} = \frac{5}{8}$
$\frac{2}{8} + \frac{4}{8} = \frac{6}{8}$	$\frac{2}{8} + \frac{6}{8} = \frac{8}{8}$	$\frac{3}{8} + \frac{1}{8} = \frac{4}{8}$	$\frac{3}{8} + \frac{2}{8} = \frac{5}{8}$
$\frac{3}{8} + \frac{3}{8} = \frac{6}{8}$	$\frac{3}{8} + \frac{4}{8} = \frac{7}{8}$	$\frac{3}{8} + \frac{5}{8} = \frac{8}{8}$	$\frac{4}{8} + \frac{1}{8} = \frac{5}{8}$
$\frac{4}{8} + \frac{4}{8} = \frac{8}{8}$	$\frac{5}{8} + \frac{2}{8} = \frac{7}{8}$	$\frac{6}{8} + \frac{1}{8} = \frac{7}{8}$	$\frac{7}{8} + \frac{1}{8} = \frac{8}{8}$

Caller Recording Chart: Adding Decimal Equivalents for $\frac{1}{2}$, $\frac{1}{4}$, and $\frac{1}{8}$ Fraction Families

$.5 + .5 = 1$	$.25 + .25 = .5$	$.25 + .5 = .75$	$.5 + .25 = .75$	$.25 + .75 = 1$	$.125 + .125 = .25$	$.125 + .25 = .375$	$.125 + .375 = .5$
$.125 + .625 = .75$	$.25 + .125 = .375$	$.25 + .25 = .5$	$.25 + .375 = .625$	$.25 + .5 = .75$	$.25 + .75 = 1$	$.375 + .125 = .5$	$.375 + .25 = .625$
$.375 + .375 = .75$	$.375 + .5 = .875$	$.375 + .625 = 1$	$.5 + .125 = .625$	$.5 + .5 = 1$	$.625 + .25 = .875$	$.75 + .125 = .875$	$.875 + .125 = 1$

Caller Recording Chart: Subtracting With Like Denominators for $\frac{1}{2}$, $\frac{1}{4}$, and $\frac{1}{8}$ Fraction Families

$\frac{2}{2} - \frac{1}{2} = \left(\frac{1}{2}\right)$	$\frac{3}{4} - \frac{1}{4} = \left(\frac{2}{4}\right)$	$\frac{3}{4} - \frac{2}{4} = \left(\frac{1}{4}\right)$	$\frac{4}{4} - \frac{1}{4} = \left(\frac{3}{4}\right)$
$\frac{8}{8} - \frac{1}{8} = \left(\frac{7}{8}\right)$	$\frac{8}{8} - \frac{2}{8} = \left(\frac{6}{8}\right)$	$\frac{8}{8} - \frac{3}{8} = \left(\frac{5}{8}\right)$	$\frac{8}{8} - \frac{5}{8} = \left(\frac{3}{8}\right)$
$\frac{7}{8} - \frac{1}{8} = \left(\frac{6}{8}\right)$	$\frac{7}{8} - \frac{3}{8} = \left(\frac{4}{8}\right)$	$\frac{7}{8} - \frac{4}{8} = \left(\frac{3}{8}\right)$	$\frac{7}{8} - \frac{6}{8} = \left(\frac{1}{8}\right)$
$\frac{6}{8} - \frac{1}{8} = \left(\frac{5}{8}\right)$	$\frac{6}{8} - \frac{2}{8} = \left(\frac{4}{8}\right)$	$\frac{6}{8} - \frac{4}{8} = \left(\frac{2}{8}\right)$	$\frac{6}{8} - \frac{5}{8} = \left(\frac{1}{8}\right)$
$\frac{5}{8} - \frac{1}{8} = \left(\frac{4}{8}\right)$	$\frac{5}{8} - \frac{3}{8} = \left(\frac{2}{8}\right)$	$\frac{5}{8} - \frac{4}{8} = \left(\frac{1}{8}\right)$	$\frac{4}{8} - \frac{1}{8} = \left(\frac{3}{8}\right)$
$\frac{4}{8} - \frac{2}{8} = \left(\frac{2}{8}\right)$	$\frac{3}{8} - \frac{1}{8} = \left(\frac{2}{8}\right)$	$\frac{3}{8} - \frac{2}{8} = \left(\frac{1}{8}\right)$	$\frac{2}{8} - \frac{1}{8} = \left(\frac{1}{8}\right)$

Caller Recording Chart: Subtracting Decimal Equivalents for $\frac{1}{2}$, $\frac{1}{4}$, and $\frac{1}{8}$ Fraction Families

$1 - .5 = (.5)$	$.75 - .25 = (.5)$	$.75 - .5 = (.25)$	$1 - .25 = (.75)$	$1 - .125 = (.875)$	$1 - .25 = (.75)$	$1 - .375 = (.625)$	$1 - .625 = (.375)$
$.875 - .125 = (.75)$	$.875 - .375 = (.5)$	$.875 - .5 = (.375)$	$.875 - .75 = (.125)$	$.75 - .125 = (.625)$	$.75 - .25 = (.5)$	$.75 - .5 = (.25)$	$.75 - .625 = (.125)$
$.625 - .125 = (.5)$	$.625 - .375 = (.25)$	$.625 - .5 = (.125)$	$.5 - .125 = (.375)$	$.5 - .25 = (.25)$	$.375 - .125 = (.25)$	$.375 - .25 = (.125)$	$.25 - .125 = (.125)$

Math Games to Master Basic Skills: Fractions & Decimals Scholastic Teaching Resources

Caller Recording Chart: Adding With Like Denominators for $\frac{1}{5}$ and $\frac{1}{10}$ Fraction Families

$\frac{1}{5} + \frac{1}{5} = \left(\frac{2}{5}\right)$	$\frac{1}{5} + \frac{2}{5} = \left(\frac{3}{5}\right)$	$\frac{2}{5} + \frac{3}{5} = \left(\frac{5}{5}\right)$	$\frac{3}{5} + \frac{1}{5} = \left(\frac{4}{5}\right)$
$\frac{4}{5} + \frac{1}{5} = \left(\frac{5}{5}\right)$	$\frac{1}{10} + \frac{1}{10} = \left(\frac{2}{10}\right)$	$\frac{1}{10} + \frac{3}{10} = \left(\frac{4}{10}\right)$	$\frac{1}{10} + \frac{4}{10} = \left(\frac{5}{10}\right)$
$\frac{1}{10} + \frac{7}{10} = \left(\frac{8}{10}\right)$	$\frac{2}{10} + \frac{1}{10} = \left(\frac{3}{10}\right)$	$\frac{2}{10} + \frac{3}{10} = \left(\frac{5}{10}\right)$	$\frac{2}{10} + \frac{5}{10} = \left(\frac{7}{10}\right)$
$\frac{3}{10} + \frac{3}{10} = \left(\frac{6}{10}\right)$	$\frac{3}{10} + \frac{5}{10} = \left(\frac{8}{10}\right)$	$\frac{3}{10} + \frac{7}{10} = \left(\frac{10}{10}\right)$	$\frac{4}{10} + \frac{3}{10} = \left(\frac{7}{10}\right)$
$\frac{4}{10} + \frac{4}{10} = \left(\frac{8}{10}\right)$	$\frac{4}{10} + \frac{5}{10} = \left(\frac{9}{10}\right)$	$\frac{5}{10} + \frac{1}{10} = \left(\frac{6}{10}\right)$	$\frac{5}{10} + \frac{5}{10} = \left(\frac{10}{10}\right)$
$\frac{6}{10} + \frac{1}{10} = \left(\frac{7}{10}\right)$	$\frac{6}{10} + \frac{3}{10} = \left(\frac{9}{10}\right)$	$\frac{7}{10} + \frac{2}{10} = \left(\frac{9}{10}\right)$	$\frac{8}{10} + \frac{2}{10} = \left(\frac{10}{10}\right)$

Caller Recording Chart: Adding Decimal Equivalents for $\frac{1}{5}$ and $\frac{1}{10}$ Fraction Families

.2 +.2 (.4)	.2 +.4 (.6)	.4 +.6 (1)	.6 +.2 (.8)	.8 +.2 (1)	.1 +.1 (.2)	.1 +.3 (.4)	.1 +.4 (.5)
.1 +.7 (.8)	.2 +.1 (.3)	.2 +.3 (.5)	.2 +.5 (.7)	.3 +.3 (.6)	.3 +.5 (.8)	.3 +.7 (1)	.4 +.3 (.7)
.4 +.4 (.8)	.4 +.5 (.9)	.5 +.1 (.6)	.5 +.5 (1)	.6 +.1 (.7)	.6 +.3 (.9)	.7 +.2 (.9)	.8 +.2 (1)

Caller Recording Chart: Subtracting With Like Denominators for $\frac{1}{5}$ and $\frac{1}{10}$ Fraction Families

$\frac{4}{5} - \frac{1}{5} = \frac{3}{5}$	$\frac{4}{5} - \frac{2}{5} = \frac{2}{5}$	$\frac{3}{5} - \frac{1}{5} = \frac{2}{5}$	$\frac{3}{5} - \frac{2}{5} = \frac{1}{5}$
$\frac{2}{5} - \frac{1}{5} = \frac{1}{5}$	$\frac{10}{10} - \frac{1}{10} = \frac{9}{10}$	$\frac{9}{10} - \frac{1}{10} = \frac{8}{10}$	$\frac{9}{10} - \frac{2}{10} = \frac{7}{10}$
$\frac{9}{10} - \frac{5}{10} = \frac{4}{10}$	$\frac{9}{10} - \frac{8}{10} = \frac{1}{10}$	$\frac{8}{10} - \frac{2}{10} = \frac{6}{10}$	$\frac{8}{10} - \frac{5}{10} = \frac{3}{10}$
$\frac{8}{10} - \frac{6}{10} = \frac{2}{10}$	$\frac{8}{10} - \frac{7}{10} = \frac{1}{10}$	$\frac{7}{10} - \frac{2}{10} = \frac{5}{10}$	$\frac{7}{10} - \frac{4}{10} = \frac{3}{10}$
$\frac{6}{10} - \frac{2}{10} = \frac{4}{10}$	$\frac{6}{10} - \frac{5}{10} = \frac{1}{10}$	$\frac{5}{10} - \frac{3}{10} = \frac{2}{10}$	$\frac{5}{10} - \frac{4}{10} = \frac{1}{10}$
$\frac{4}{10} - \frac{1}{10} = \frac{3}{10}$	$\frac{4}{10} - \frac{2}{10} = \frac{2}{10}$	$\frac{3}{10} - \frac{1}{10} = \frac{2}{10}$	$\frac{2}{10} - \frac{1}{10} = \frac{1}{10}$

Caller Recording Chart: Subtracting Decimal Equivalents for $\frac{1}{5}$ and $\frac{1}{10}$ Fraction Families

.8 − .2 = .6	.8 − .4 = .4	.6 − .2 = .4	.6 − .4 = .2	.4 − .2 = .2	1 − .1 = .9	.9 − .1 = .8	.9 − .2 = .7
.9 − .5 = .4	.9 − .8 = .1	.8 − .2 = .6	.8 − .5 = .3	.8 − .6 = .2	.8 − .7 = .1	.7 − .2 = .5	.7 − .4 = .3
.6 − .2 = .4	.6 − .5 = .1	.5 − .3 = .2	.5 − .4 = .1	.4 − .1 = .3	.4 − .2 = .2	.3 − .1 = .2	.2 − .1 = .1

Math Games to Master Basic Skills: Fractions & Decimals Scholastic Teaching Resources

Caller Recording Chart: Adding With Like Denominators for $\frac{1}{3}$, $\frac{1}{6}$, and $\frac{1}{9}$ Fraction Families

$\frac{1}{3} + \frac{1}{3} = \left(\frac{2}{3}\right)$	$\frac{2}{3} + \frac{1}{3} = \left(\frac{3}{3}\right)$	$\frac{1}{6} + \frac{1}{6} = \left(\frac{2}{6}\right)$	$\frac{1}{6} + \frac{2}{6} = \left(\frac{3}{6}\right)$
$\frac{1}{6} + \frac{4}{6} = \left(\frac{5}{6}\right)$	$\frac{2}{6} + \frac{2}{6} = \left(\frac{4}{6}\right)$	$\frac{2}{6} + \frac{3}{6} = \left(\frac{5}{6}\right)$	$\frac{3}{6} + \frac{1}{6} = \left(\frac{4}{6}\right)$
$\frac{4}{6} + \frac{2}{6} = \left(\frac{6}{6}\right)$	$\frac{5}{6} + \frac{1}{6} = \left(\frac{6}{6}\right)$	$\frac{1}{9} + \frac{1}{9} = \left(\frac{2}{9}\right)$	$\frac{1}{9} + \frac{2}{9} = \left(\frac{3}{9}\right)$
$\frac{1}{9} + \frac{3}{9} = \left(\frac{4}{9}\right)$	$\frac{1}{9} + \frac{5}{9} = \left(\frac{6}{9}\right)$	$\frac{2}{9} + \frac{3}{9} = \left(\frac{5}{9}\right)$	$\frac{2}{9} + \frac{4}{9} = \left(\frac{6}{9}\right)$
$\frac{2}{9} + \frac{6}{9} = \left(\frac{8}{9}\right)$	$\frac{3}{9} + \frac{1}{9} = \left(\frac{4}{9}\right)$	$\frac{3}{9} + \frac{3}{9} = \left(\frac{6}{9}\right)$	$\frac{3}{9} + \frac{5}{9} = \left(\frac{8}{9}\right)$
$\frac{4}{9} + \frac{1}{9} = \left(\frac{5}{9}\right)$	$\frac{4}{9} + \frac{5}{9} = \left(\frac{9}{9}\right)$	$\frac{5}{9} + \frac{2}{9} = \left(\frac{7}{9}\right)$	$\frac{6}{9} + \frac{3}{9} = \left(\frac{9}{9}\right)$

Caller Recording Chart: Subtracting With Like Denominators for $\frac{1}{3}$, $\frac{1}{6}$, and $\frac{1}{9}$ Fraction Families

$\frac{2}{3} - \frac{1}{3} = \left(\frac{1}{3}\right)$	$\frac{3}{3} - \frac{1}{3} = \left(\frac{2}{3}\right)$	$\frac{6}{6} - \frac{1}{6} = \left(\frac{5}{6}\right)$	$\frac{6}{6} - \frac{2}{6} = \left(\frac{4}{6}\right)$
$\frac{5}{6} - \frac{1}{6} = \left(\frac{4}{6}\right)$	$\frac{5}{6} - \frac{2}{6} = \left(\frac{3}{6}\right)$	$\frac{4}{6} - \frac{1}{6} = \left(\frac{3}{6}\right)$	$\frac{3}{6} - \frac{1}{6} = \left(\frac{2}{6}\right)$
$\frac{2}{6} - \frac{1}{6} = \left(\frac{1}{6}\right)$	$\frac{9}{9} - \frac{1}{9} = \left(\frac{8}{9}\right)$	$\frac{9}{9} - \frac{4}{9} = \left(\frac{5}{9}\right)$	$\frac{9}{9} - \frac{5}{9} = \left(\frac{4}{9}\right)$
$\frac{8}{9} - \frac{1}{9} = \left(\frac{7}{9}\right)$	$\frac{8}{9} - \frac{2}{9} = \left(\frac{6}{9}\right)$	$\frac{8}{9} - \frac{4}{9} = \left(\frac{4}{9}\right)$	$\frac{7}{9} - \frac{1}{9} = \left(\frac{6}{9}\right)$
$\frac{7}{9} - \frac{2}{9} = \left(\frac{5}{9}\right)$	$\frac{6}{9} - \frac{1}{9} = \left(\frac{5}{9}\right)$	$\frac{6}{9} - \frac{3}{9} = \left(\frac{3}{9}\right)$	$\frac{5}{9} - \frac{1}{9} = \left(\frac{4}{9}\right)$
$\frac{5}{9} - \frac{2}{9} = \left(\frac{3}{9}\right)$	$\frac{4}{9} - \frac{1}{9} = \left(\frac{3}{9}\right)$	$\frac{4}{9} - \frac{2}{9} = \left(\frac{2}{9}\right)$	$\frac{3}{9} - \frac{2}{9} = \left(\frac{1}{9}\right)$

Caller Recording Chart: Adding With Like Denominators for $\frac{1}{100}$ and $\frac{1}{1000}$ Fraction Families

$\frac{1}{100} + \frac{1}{100} = \left(\frac{2}{100}\right)$	$\frac{1}{100} + \frac{3}{100} = \left(\frac{4}{100}\right)$	$\frac{2}{100} + \frac{1}{100} = \left(\frac{3}{100}\right)$	$\frac{2}{100} + \frac{5}{100} = \left(\frac{7}{100}\right)$
$\frac{3}{100} + \frac{2}{100} = \left(\frac{5}{100}\right)$	$\frac{3}{100} + \frac{4}{100} = \left(\frac{7}{100}\right)$	$\frac{4}{100} + \frac{2}{100} = \left(\frac{6}{100}\right)$	$\frac{5}{100} + \frac{3}{100} = \left(\frac{8}{100}\right)$
$\frac{6}{100} + \frac{3}{100} = \left(\frac{9}{100}\right)$	$\frac{7}{100} + \frac{1}{100} = \left(\frac{8}{100}\right)$	$\frac{8}{100} + \frac{1}{100} = \left(\frac{9}{100}\right)$	$\frac{25}{100} + \frac{75}{100} = \left(\frac{100}{100}\right)$
$\frac{1}{1000} + \frac{1}{1000} = \left(\frac{2}{1000}\right)$	$\frac{1}{1000} + \frac{3}{1000} = \left(\frac{4}{1000}\right)$	$\frac{2}{1000} + \frac{1}{1000} = \left(\frac{3}{1000}\right)$	$\frac{2}{1000} + \frac{5}{1000} = \left(\frac{7}{1000}\right)$
$\frac{3}{1000} + \frac{2}{1000} = \left(\frac{5}{1000}\right)$	$\frac{3}{1000} + \frac{4}{1000} = \left(\frac{7}{1000}\right)$	$\frac{4}{1000} + \frac{2}{1000} = \left(\frac{6}{1000}\right)$	$\frac{4}{1000} + \frac{5}{1000} = \left(\frac{9}{1000}\right)$
$\frac{5}{1000} + \frac{1}{1000} = \left(\frac{6}{1000}\right)$	$\frac{5}{1000} + \frac{3}{1000} = \left(\frac{8}{1000}\right)$	$\frac{6}{1000} + \frac{2}{1000} = \left(\frac{8}{1000}\right)$	$\frac{900}{1000} + \frac{100}{1000} = \left(\frac{1000}{1000}\right)$

Caller Recording Chart: Adding Decimal Equivalents for $\frac{1}{100}$ and $\frac{1}{1000}$ Fraction Families

.01 +.01 (.02)	.01 +.03 (.04)	.02 +.01 (.03)	.02 +.05 (.07)	.03 +.02 (.05)	.03 +.04 (.07)	.04 +.02 (.06)	.05 +.03 (.08)
.06 +.03 (.09)	.07 +.01 (.08)	.08 +.01 (.09)	.25 +.75 (1)	.001 +.001 (.002)	.001 +.003 (.004)	.002 +.001 (.003)	.002 +.005 (.007)
.003 +.002 (.005)	.003 +.004 (.007)	.004 +.002 (.006)	.004 +.005 (.009)	.005 +.001 (.006)	.005 +.003 (.008)	.006 +.002 (.008)	.900 +.100 (1)

Math Games to Master Basic Skills: Fractions & Decimals Scholastic Teaching Resources

Caller Recording Chart: Subtracting With Like Denominators for $\frac{1}{100}$ and $\frac{1}{1000}$ Fraction Families

$\frac{10}{100} - \frac{1}{100} = \left(\frac{9}{100}\right)$	$\frac{9}{100} - \frac{1}{100} = \left(\frac{8}{100}\right)$	$\frac{9}{100} - \frac{2}{100} = \left(\frac{7}{100}\right)$	$\frac{8}{100} - \frac{2}{100} = \left(\frac{6}{100}\right)$
$\frac{8}{100} - \frac{4}{100} = \left(\frac{4}{100}\right)$	$\frac{7}{100} - \frac{3}{100} = \left(\frac{4}{100}\right)$	$\frac{6}{100} - \frac{1}{100} = \left(\frac{5}{100}\right)$	$\frac{6}{100} - \frac{5}{100} = \left(\frac{1}{100}\right)$
$\frac{5}{100} - \frac{2}{100} = \left(\frac{3}{100}\right)$	$\frac{4}{100} - \frac{3}{100} = \left(\frac{1}{100}\right)$	$\frac{3}{100} - \frac{1}{100} = \left(\frac{2}{100}\right)$	$\frac{2}{100} - \frac{1}{100} = \left(\frac{1}{100}\right)$
$\frac{10}{1000} - \frac{1}{1000} = \left(\frac{9}{1000}\right)$	$\frac{9}{1000} - \frac{1}{1000} = \left(\frac{8}{1000}\right)$	$\frac{9}{1000} - \frac{3}{1000} = \left(\frac{6}{1000}\right)$	$\frac{8}{1000} - \frac{1}{1000} = \left(\frac{7}{1000}\right)$
$\frac{8}{1000} - \frac{5}{1000} = \left(\frac{3}{1000}\right)$	$\frac{7}{1000} - \frac{2}{1000} = \left(\frac{5}{1000}\right)$	$\frac{7}{1000} - \frac{5}{1000} = \left(\frac{2}{1000}\right)$	$\frac{6}{1000} - \frac{2}{1000} = \left(\frac{4}{1000}\right)$
$\frac{5}{1000} - \frac{2}{1000} = \left(\frac{3}{1000}\right)$	$\frac{4}{1000} - \frac{3}{1000} = \left(\frac{1}{1000}\right)$	$\frac{3}{1000} - \frac{1}{1000} = \left(\frac{2}{1000}\right)$	$\frac{2}{1000} - \frac{1}{1000} = \left(\frac{1}{1000}\right)$

Caller Recording Chart: Subtracting Decimal Equivalents for $\frac{1}{100}$ and $\frac{1}{1000}$ Fraction Families

$.1 - .01 = (.09)$	$.09 - .01 = (.08)$	$.09 - .02 = (.07)$	$.08 - .02 = (.06)$	$.08 - .04 = (.04)$	$.07 - .03 = (.04)$	$.06 - .01 = (.05)$	$.06 - .05 = (.01)$
$.05 - .02 = (.03)$	$.04 - .03 = (.01)$	$.03 - .01 = (.02)$	$.02 - .01 = (.01)$	$.01 - .001 = (.009)$	$.009 - .001 = (.008)$	$.009 - .003 = (.006)$	$.008 - .001 = (.007)$
$.008 - .005 = (.003)$	$.007 - .002 = (.005)$	$.007 - .005 = (.002)$	$.006 - .002 = (.004)$	$.005 - .002 = (.003)$	$.004 - .003 = (.001)$	$.003 - .001 = (.002)$	$.002 - .001 = (.001)$

PLAYER 1

$\dfrac{1}{3} + \dfrac{1}{9} =$	$\dfrac{5}{8} - \dfrac{1}{4} =$	$\dfrac{1}{4} + \dfrac{5}{8} =$	$\dfrac{1}{2} + \dfrac{3}{8} =$
$\dfrac{7}{8} - \dfrac{1}{4} =$	$\dfrac{1}{3} + \dfrac{2}{6} =$	$\dfrac{6}{9} + \dfrac{1}{3} =$	$\dfrac{1}{8} + \dfrac{1}{4} =$
$\dfrac{2}{3} - \dfrac{3}{6} =$	$\dfrac{1}{8} + \dfrac{3}{4} =$	$\dfrac{1}{6} + \dfrac{1}{2} =$	$\dfrac{3}{4} - \dfrac{1}{2} =$
$\dfrac{1}{3} + \dfrac{4}{9} =$	$\dfrac{4}{6} - \dfrac{1}{3} =$	$\dfrac{2}{5} + \dfrac{1}{5} =$	$\dfrac{2}{9} + \dfrac{2}{3} =$
$\dfrac{4}{5} - \dfrac{1}{5} =$	$\dfrac{5}{6} - \dfrac{1}{3} =$	$\dfrac{1}{3} - \dfrac{1}{6} =$	$\dfrac{2}{10} + \dfrac{1}{5} =$
$\dfrac{3}{10} + \dfrac{1}{2} =$	$\dfrac{1}{2} + \dfrac{4}{8} =$	$\dfrac{5}{8} - \dfrac{1}{2} =$	$\dfrac{2}{3} + \dfrac{2}{6} =$
$\dfrac{4}{9} - \dfrac{1}{3} =$	$\dfrac{8}{9} - \dfrac{1}{3} =$	$\dfrac{2}{5} - \dfrac{1}{5} =$	$\dfrac{2}{3} + \dfrac{1}{9} =$
$\dfrac{3}{4} - \dfrac{1}{8} =$	$\dfrac{4}{9} - \dfrac{2}{9} =$	$\dfrac{7}{8} - \dfrac{3}{4} =$	$\dfrac{3}{4} - \dfrac{5}{8} =$

Math Games to Master Basic Skills: Fractions & Decimals Scholastic Teaching Resources

Checkers Game Board: Fractions

$\frac{1}{2} + \frac{1}{4} =$	$\frac{3}{5} + \frac{2}{5} =$	$\frac{1}{8} + \frac{1}{2} =$	$\frac{4}{9} + \frac{5}{9} =$
$\frac{6}{8} - \frac{1}{2} =$	$\frac{1}{5} + \frac{3}{5} =$	$\frac{1}{2} + \frac{2}{8} =$	$\frac{4}{5} - \frac{6}{10} =$
$\frac{1}{6} + \frac{2}{3} =$	$\frac{2}{6} - \frac{1}{3} =$	$\frac{1}{4} - \frac{1}{8} =$	$\frac{6}{9} - \frac{1}{3} =$
$\frac{1}{8} + \frac{5}{8} =$	$\frac{1}{3} + \frac{1}{3} =$	$\frac{2}{4} - \frac{1}{2} =$	$\frac{3}{5} - \frac{1}{5} =$
$\frac{2}{3} - \frac{1}{3} =$	$\frac{3}{4} - \frac{3}{8} =$	$\frac{1}{3} + \frac{2}{3} =$	$\frac{7}{8} - \frac{1}{2} =$
$\frac{1}{10} + \frac{3}{5} =$	$\frac{4}{9} + \frac{1}{9} =$	$\frac{4}{5} - \frac{3}{5} =$	$\frac{7}{9} - \frac{2}{9} =$
$\frac{1}{4} + \frac{1}{2} =$	$\frac{1}{2} - \frac{1}{4} =$	$\frac{3}{4} + \frac{1}{8} =$	$\frac{4}{5} + \frac{1}{5} =$
$\frac{5}{8} - \frac{1}{2} =$	$\frac{6}{10} + \frac{1}{5} =$	$\frac{9}{10} - \frac{4}{5} =$	$\frac{1}{8} + \frac{1}{2} =$

PLAYER 2

Glue here.

Checkers Game Board: Decimals

.3 − .1 =	.4 + .125 =	.1 + .125 =	1 − .875 =
.1 + .2 =	.125 − .1 =	.5 + .5 =	.6 − .5 =
.75 + .03 =	.4 + .25 =	.5 − .1 =	.005 + .005 =
.375 − .25 =	.4 + .375 =	.2 − .2 =	.375 + .2 =
.875 − .5 =	.2 − .005 =	.75 − .3 =	.4 − .375 =
.1 + .2 =	.09 + .9 =	.825 − .375 =	.9 + .1 =
.125 + .05 =	.3 − .1 =	.75 + .05 =	.6 − .125 =
.25 + .25 =	.5 − .25 =	.005 + .125 =	.5 − .375 =

PLAYER 1

Math Games to Master Basic Skills: Fractions & Decimals Scholastic Teaching Resources

Checkers Game Board: Decimals

.8 − .625 =	.04 − .02 =	.8 + .2 =	.04 − .004 =
.05 + .05 =	.125 − .02 =	.02 + .03 =	.9 − .5 =
.125 + .375 =	.1 − .05 =	.1 + .025 =	.8 − .25 =
.4 − .3 =	.004 + .003 =	.25 + .25 =	.08 − .075 =
.06 + .03 =	.001 + .008 =	.9 − .4 =	.875 − .03 =
.01 + .05 =	.2 + .6 =	.5 − .125 =	.005 + .025 =
.2 − .05 =	.25 + .6 =	.5 + .25 =	.9 − .025 =
.125 + .5 =	.1 + .05 =	.5 − .4 =	.625 − .25 =

PLAYER 2

Glue here.

Fraction Checkers Answer Key

$\frac{4}{9}$	$\frac{3}{8}$	$\frac{7}{8}$	$\frac{7}{8}$	$\frac{3}{4}$	1	$\frac{5}{8}$	1
$\frac{5}{8}$	$\frac{2}{3}$	1	$\frac{3}{8}$	$\frac{1}{4}$	$\frac{4}{5}$	$\frac{3}{4}$	$\frac{1}{5}$
$\frac{1}{6}$	$\frac{7}{8}$	$\frac{2}{3}$	$\frac{1}{4}$	$\frac{5}{6}$	0	$\frac{1}{8}$	$\frac{1}{3}$
$\frac{7}{9}$	$\frac{1}{3}$	$\frac{3}{5}$	$\frac{8}{9}$	$\frac{3}{4}$	$\frac{2}{3}$	0	$\frac{2}{5}$
$\frac{3}{5}$	$\frac{1}{2}$	$\frac{1}{6}$	$\frac{2}{5}$	$\frac{1}{3}$	$\frac{3}{8}$	1	$\frac{3}{8}$
$\frac{4}{5}$	1	$\frac{1}{8}$	1	$\frac{7}{10}$	$\frac{5}{9}$	$\frac{1}{5}$	$\frac{5}{9}$
$\frac{1}{9}$	$\frac{5}{9}$	$\frac{1}{5}$	$\frac{7}{9}$	$\frac{3}{4}$	$\frac{1}{4}$	$\frac{7}{8}$	1
$\frac{5}{8}$	$\frac{2}{9}$	$\frac{1}{8}$	$\frac{1}{8}$	$\frac{1}{8}$	$\frac{4}{5}$	$\frac{1}{10}$	$\frac{5}{8}$

PLAYER 1   PLAYER 2

Decimal Checkers Answer Key

.2	.525	.225	.125	.175	.02	1	.036
.3	.025	1	.1	.1	.105	.05	.4
.78	.65	.4	.01	.5	.05	.125	.55
.125	.775	0	.575	.1	.007	.5	.005
.375	.195	.45	.025	.09	.009	.5	.845
.3	.99	.45	1	.06	.8	.375	.03
.175	.2	.8	.475	.15	.85	.75	.875
.5	.25	.13	.125	.625	.15	.1	.375

PLAYER 1   PLAYER 2

Math Games to Master Basic Skills: Fractions & Decimals Scholastic Teaching Resources